Ah there is so much to do but yet the spirit is weak; becoming weaker day by day.

I see life but yet it feels like there is no life within me.

The spirit is down; feels like it's dying for some strange reason.

There is no one I can talk to about this because none can comprehend this. To some it's all in my mind but who feels it knows it.

Do I want to run and hide?

Not run and hide, but go somewhere where there is lots of sun. At times my body feels cold and all it requires is heat, heat to rejuvenate and live.

Limitations are there and trust me I am limited and this is sad. Sad to know and sad to live but this is my life. I have to live it regardless of my limitations and draining energy. Yes the body has strength but yet it's weak being drained.

Is there a better way to explain this?

No, not without confusing you and you are already confused. Certain things you have to go through and trust me I am going through it and going through it alone.

Should anyone go through this?

No, but the reality is, **there are wicked and evil people and spirits out there that does hurt.** Some people don't care who they hurt as long as they get what they want. Like I've told you in my book My Many Questions To God, **this woman tied me. I should not have anything in life. I was to end up begging in the streets with my children.** It almost happened. I'm still fighting financially and can't go anymore. This is my reality when it comes to the evils of man and spirit; hence I know the wickedness and evils of man and spirit.

You do not have to do anything to anyone for them to hurt you. A person can just look at you and not like you.

Some of us see the evils of them and some don't.

If you are a good person with a good heart evil and wicked people will not like you. They will do all to destroy you; kill you.

They will do all for you to fail.

Is this right?

No, hence I tell Good God I will not tell anyone to follow him nor will I forgive her for tying me. I did her nothing and she did all to take everything from me with her evil. Yes I know the road of hardship and pain that I am on and I would not wish this road for my worst enemy. I did not choose this road but yet he Good God has and have allowed evil to penetrate my world and caused me anger and pain. As someone I more than truly love, I am expecting him to be my more than protector against all that is wicked and evil. Yes my mind is telling me I had to go through this because he Good God needed me to shut all facets of evil down infinitely and indefinitely forever ever without end. But in knowing this fam, I truly don't feel better. Evil should not penetrate Good God's world and worlds in the first place. His people are his people and evil should infinitely and indefinitely never ever come around them or near them.

Evil cannot change he knows this and so do I; hence evil take what do not belong to them. Fam, evil should not even be on the same planet with Good God's children and people come on now.

So because of this I will not tell anyone to follow him Good God because I know the unfair treatment his people get. **_To me if you have to go throw this; such pain and heartache there is no truth or justice in him. And yes this is my anger speaking on this day because in order for you to shut down evil you have to know evil and go through evil so that others don't have to. Meaning you are the one to make a better way for you and your people; the seeds and or people he Good God has and_** *have given you to rescue; save. Yes I have a lot of these negative days. These days I loathe and yes it's unfortunate that I have to go through them alone.*

Damn I should write my own prescription for these awful and depressing days.

Do I enjoy the life I am living?

Truthfully, not on days like these. Trust me, I would rather be sitting on the beach somewhere enjoying the sea and sea breeze whilst listening to Total Praise by Fred Hammond, and writing songs of devotion and truth to Good God.

Yes the environment I'm in would be totally peaceful because none of my children would be allowed to live with me. I need my own world where I am totally devoted to my one true love and that is to Good God and my more than wonderful and gorgeous mummy; mother. Man do I miss her and wish I could see her each and every day. I would hug her and kiss her and tell her how much I truly loved her. Yes I am smiling as I think of her. So yes with every ounce of my being I have to save her.

Listen fam, when I truly love I truly love to the point where people will hate me. I truly love to show affection my way not the way someone tells me to. Yes I spoil hence I have to spoil my gorgeous mother. Trust me no universe is too good for her. And yes I get Good God jealous with the way I speak of my mother because he is a jealous god but not as jealous as me. I am more jealous than him and fiercer as well; hence I am the female Lyon come on now.

Are others capable of this truth?

We all are. Some just prefer to tell lies and live by lies that's all and I cannot do this. I have to live for me and the truth that is in me. Yes I live by Good God as well but I truly have to live for me and do all that I can in goodness and truth to preserve good and true life including the seeds he Good God has and have given me.

We all belong but evil; wicked and evil people including spirits want it all, so they do all to destroy all that is good and true.

<u>Everything with evil is about prophet whoops profit; money.</u>

I am not saying it's bad to have money, it isn't. It's the greed (man or woman including child) behind the money is what's evil.

As humans we do not buy to preserve or replant. As humans we do all to destroy; kill including spread hate.

Look at the environment that we live in. Is it necessary to pollute the environment; air and waterways including soil so much?

We do not care but yet we want God to care. If he Good God has and have given us something beautiful why destroy it?

We need to keep all that he's given us clean including self.

Like I've said in some of my other books, Good God cannot come into a dirty planet and the more we sin is the farther he gets from us. Truly look at earth and the bloodletting that we as humans do. Can Good God come into this planet and be with us when it's so dirty?

No right?

So why do we keep hindering him?

Why do we cause him pain?

Why do we keep everything dirty including self?

I've hurt him but now I am learning not to. Yes I know I had to go through this because evil does not want the truth to be known. Evil and or Sin does not want to lose anyone; so evil does all to keep self, land, seas, and planet including universe dirty. When sin do this, Good

God cannot enter. Hence I've told you evil won over man in 2013.

Humans are not loyal beings.

Stop it Joe because if you say it I will blast you. Your sins – humanities sins are there as a living testament.

Did you not cheat on your wife recently? So shut up because you know what I am talking about. Our sins are negatives not positives.

So as negative energy grows so does our sins.

But, but nothing. Think of it as being a part of the collective; your chosen society then.

But you are so racist and you shouldn't talk.

Well kiss my ass because I can talk. And Fred stop laughing. Take your hand from your mouth because I am so not the typical writer. I tell you like it is and if you don't like it too damn bad. You have a stove, burn the book, throw it against the wall. Yes I know you're going to kill me because many of you are saying "I am going to kill you."

See now this is where I would get angry with the killing bullshit, but I am going to reserve my anger for now.

Cussed her out somewhat in the book My Many Questions To God already, so I will not cuss you for now.

Some of you may be asking why not e-books. Never will like e-books or e-pubs. People when you can throw a book, you can't throw your expensive machines. Yes I want you to throw these books if I upset you. Throw them if you are annoyed at me, then go back and read the message after you have calmed down.

And yes you can read other people's materials, books. I truly love historical romances and I so have to get back into them so that I can promote other writers.

Living clean does not mean giving up on life people come on now.

Do I want to take some belly dancing classes?

Yes I do, but African Belly Dance.

My hips I truly love to move people; hence walking is on my agenda to do when the weather gets better.

Man I have to get some book marks that has 2-3 pages on them for you to make notes. Yes you have to make notes with the page numbers so that when you see me you say, Michelle in Blackman Redemption you said this,

this and this. I do not understand please clarify. You guys are my book marks and students. Yeah me!!!!

Yes I look forward to this.

Do I want to fill up stadiums?

Yeah, we have to have coffee or tea with our bagel or croissant. Think of it as Michelle's happy party. Crony yes but true. Why wouldn't I want to have fun with all of you?

Some of you take me to bed anyway. And you better.

Hey I need my nightly hugs and kisses.

Damn now I need you to wrap your arms and legs around me. Ah yes my big breasts, well chest.

Yes you can lay your head on my chest. Ah let me rub your head and say dear, dear. Feel better?

How was your day?

Was it stressful?

Yes.

Okay, let me make you a coffee and put a rose on the table just for you.

Come let me hug and kiss you. Tell you I am there for you always and I truly, truly love you. Take my hand, feel my energy because you are truly loved more than forever ever by me.

Come on yes you, take me because we are so kicking it old school. Yeah baby crank up Lloyd's Lay it Down because it's my pillow you're on and my pillows are freshly scented with a hint of Musk and Jasmine. Yes it's a powerful combination if you know what I mean. So come on baby LAY IT DOWN.

Yes this is me and I truly hope you love me too. So no jealousy because you have me all to yourself on your given days.

No I'm not you are saying because you have to share me.

I know you don't want to share me but you have to. It's nothing sexual because true love isn't about sexual gratification, it's about truth, happiness and positive growth. There, smile for me because you are a part of my good and true universe and world. So come on Lay it Down. You truly have me. This is our little romance that cannot fade; die so lay it down.

Come on baby I know you don't want to share me, but I'm sharing you. And don't you dare say it, because we are not cheating, true families don't cheat. Cheating is nasty and you know this so tell her about me. Tell him about me.

Yeah I'm going to sit in your lap and his too hence I am practicing what I preach. So truly don't talk s**t. Hey the ass is clean so don't go there. Laugh because I know you are laughing up a storm. Yes I went there, and remember we are UNCONDITIONAL Rueben Studdard. Hey you have me unconditional what more is there to say.

Feeling better now?

Yes.

Then I've done my job on this day, **_and yes THE STORM IS OVER NOW R. Kelly._** I am with you and hey we will have our own connection someday. Remember, I am there for you no matter the storm and storms that come your way. I am on twitter but I am getting annoyed with twitter for some strange reason, hence I want to delete my account but I won't because you need me and you are depending on me. Yes the rain is there, the sun does not shine on you. This is your thought, but the sun shines on you because I am your true light, the one that is there for you through thick or thin despite your heartache and pain. I can feel your hurt so let me dry your tears and lead you home. It matters not if you are sick like me, I am there for you.

It matters not if you are going through financial difficulties like me, I am there for you and with you. We will get through this together as more than true friends and true love. My true love for you is there, so take some and heal you no matter your healing. It's there to give so truly take what you need and leave the rest from someone else; others that need me. Touch me and feel me because I know you can. Enjoy me while you can.

Your pain does not have to be. In our world of truth, there is none; no pain. There is help hence I am with you; there for you. And as I stretch my hand to you, take it and never let go because I will never ever intentionally hurt you. True love is rare darling and it does not hurt. So when someone is giving you truth and true love unconditionally, hold on to that person and cherish them. Hey, look at me and Good God, how I more than truly love him unconditionally. At times I am obsessed with him, hence I project my more than true love of him to him and in these books so you can see and feel. **_True can never fail but lies fail and hurt._** So come on, take my hand and never let go. We need each other and this is my true outlet to you and Good God.

No I refuse to have Facebook. No even if you were to give me all the money on earth would I have Facebook ever again. Nope, nope, nope.

Don't even look for me on Instagram because I am not a social networking person. I need one outlet and one outlet alone for me and you and one day I will have it.
Yes I am a dinosaur and I live in the dinosaur age and I truly love it. Technology is too advanced hence it cannot truly find me. Yes I miss the days of the typewriter. I don't know but I think humans have become so advanced that we do not know how to interact positively with each other anymore.

We've become such attention slores that many will do anything for attention. Yes this is sad hence technology is so not for me. I am not free with technology. Yes I own a TV John. I use it as my computer monitor.

Do not forget, I truly do not have cable or satellite. Funny, the most television I watched in the longest while was when I was in LA with my brother.

But, but. No but, buts. I'm one that could write 24/7. I am more than passionate about writing. Yes there are days when I get bored and want to do something on a whim. Trust me if I could afford to do so I would but I can't.

I truly love to travel on my terms not on someone else's.

I truly love to walk but yet where I am I cannot truly walk. I have to have someone with me but in LA, man oh man I don't need anyone to walk with me. I truly love going about by myself. As long as I know where to go I am fine. Maybe that's why I dream about LA so much. I am free to do whatever I want to do without restrictions and limitations. No I am limited but I can go places by myself. I can walk by myself like I've said. Plus LA reminds me of Jamaica so I am truly not missing anything there. I am right at home.

And no I still wouldn't live in LA. LA is a booty call and or business for me. Maybe that's why it's called California. You fornicate rude there.

Yes I am missing there but can't go back.

Ah yes the South does something for me and no I still don't want to save there even if my spirit is saying otherwise on this day. I don't know people but my spirit is having compassion for a land that is sinful and evil.

Maybe it's the upright triangle that they house and the many homeless that I have compassion for. Yes I want to go there and feed these people, provide for them. My heart aches to see so much people without food and shelter.

It's not oh but Michelle. I know what it feels like to not have food. I know what it's like to feel hopeless and destitute. **THIS IS WHY I TELL YOU, GOOD GOD DOES NOT LOCK ANYONE OUT OF HIS**

KINGDOM AND ABODE; WE ARE THE ONES TO LOCK OURSELVES OUT WITH OUR SINS.

<u>Life isn`t about unhealthy living, it`s about healthy and clean living come on now.</u>

Good God is there for us all but we are the ones that`s not there for him and this is truly sad.

Yes billions can be saved but do they want or need to? It's not up to me to save them. I can only save Good God's true people if I am the saving grace from humanity. Like I've said, I will not save anyone that is wicked and evil and this goes for wicked and evil spirits. Hence Mother Earth Africa told me she's tired and asked for prayer and prayer was granted to her.

The universe is tired. He wants to get rid of him hence in all that I do I have to remember Mother Africa and the Universe. I have to pray for them because no one likes to live in mess; an environment that is unhealthy and unclean; an environment that cause hurt and pain come on now.

Michelle Jean

It's March 21, 2015 and I've had some weird dreams this morning. The one that stand out the most is the one of Tim Duncan. Family this dream is so odd that I truly do not know what to make of it. Hence I will try not to make any comments nor will I try to decipher this dream because this is one for the record books to me.

Dreamt I was somewhere where there was a river – water, and Tim Duncan all of a sudden took my hand and we were running through the water. At first the water looked foggy but there was no fog because the water was clear; you could see the fish in the water. The running we were running, I saw the fishes in the water and family I've never seen such ugly fishes in my life. Di fish dem uglier than Parana's and or the ugliest fish in the bottom of the sea. Some of the fishes had different colours but the main and or outer part of the fish was black. Dem black an ugly. I said to him if he was going to protect me and di man tell mi no. Fam, the fishes to me looked dangerous as if they would attack me, an mi ask di blasted man if im would protect me and im tell mi noa. Wha kine a man wey tek a oman han anna run wid har inna dangerous water and naah protect har?

Well suffice it to say, I was not bit by any of the fish and I made it to my destination okay. But his mom, this black woman in the dream also took my hand and was with me in the water. She kept smiling at him as if she was happy with me. The same route Tim and I took in the water we took and came back to their house. While back

Tim went up the stairs to his bedroom and I followed him. Going up the stairs I saw his sister. She had fair skin and she was pretty with nice long hair. She was not fat but skinny meaning she had a beautiful shape. I saw her and she saw me but we said nothing to each other.

Going to Tim's room his furniture was old, so old it looked broken down. He sat on the bed and I wanted to take a shower to wash the salt water off me and I asked him if I could take a shower and he told me no. I guess he did not want his mother to get the wrong impression because I was in his room and I thought we were going to do the nasty. And no, we did not get it on because his mom was in the house. While I was in the room I think she came upstairs and I ended up putting lotion on his feet. Fam, the man had the tiniest feet in the dream. He had hairy feet but tiny feet for a tall guy. To me this was odd for such a tall man to have such tiny feet.

I think I know what the feet part means but I am not one hundred percent sure. I want to comment but I won't. He has to watch his feet I guess. But as for the fishes – these ugly fishes, I truly don't know what it means. I know fish means pregnancy but so much fishes of black and multicoloured that's truly ugly, I truly do not know. I've never seen such ugly fishes before though. Hence I am so going to leave this dream alone.

Also dreaming about children. I can't remember my dream fully so I will leave this dream alone also.

MY TALK

Yes I need to do some house cleaning hence I dreamt I was buying sunlight and or laundry detergent. I was also at the laundry mat washing my clothes, so I have to get my laundry done and clean up my house because it is dirty. Too much crap happening to me since I came back from LA, hence I truly have to kick some of my children out. They are of the age when they can be on their own. And don't any of you dare say anything because I uphold too much slackness when it comes to them and it has to stop. I cannot be doing whilst grown ass children sit at home and do nothing. My first son is different hence he's excluded from the rest of the pact. He's ambitious and he does think of his mother in many ways; the rest are just stress. Too damned stressful and I truly can't take the stress anymore.

Like I told my sister, when I am gone I am outta here. Meaning as soon as I get my opening and these books start selling, trust me I am so gone and none can come say Mama I am coming with you apart from my oldest son. All others can chuck because dem no listen to good council. My first will forever ever have a saving grace with me because if I had my last penny and he needed it I would give it to him. Family, if you have a good child that tries and help you, reward them in goodness and in truth. Trust me, Good God and Allelujah don't have to ask who I would save amongst my children if push comes to shove. He would be the first one. Not because he's my first child but because he is there for me through sickness and in health. When I got sick he stood up and took charge of everything. He was my feet when I could hardly walk. He still is until this day. Hence I am more than proud of him. I have to make a way for him. So yes I would take him and only him. The rest can go. The rest truly don't listen and they've caused me too much stress and heartache in my life. As a parent you are telling them things for their own good and they are telling me dem nah listen to yu. So listen to yourself because when I am gone I won't be there, and truss mi dem a guh feel it. Yes I want and need to move to someplace warm and Cayman Islands I am coming home. This is where Good God and Allelujah wants me to be hence I have to listen and do what he tells me to do.

Yes it's crazy fam but this is my reality. I need to be at peace and rest and I will be.

I have to do what makes me happy now and shortly I will rise.

Like I said, in my other book, I will never ever forgive her for tying me.

He tied me and she tied me, hence I make no provision more than infinitely and indefinitely forever ever without end for anyone who is wicked and evil. Let hell be their home because wickedness does not pay.

You do not hurt people come on now. I've done you nothing but you tied me. You tied me so that I would not prosper. I would end up begging in the streets. What did I do to you for you to willingly do this to me?

This also brings me to one of my dreams this morning where I was saying there is no God because he allows shit to happen to his people. We are depending on him for security but we are not secure in him because he cannot protect us. He allows evil to conquer and divide; break us. **Yes I know there is a god, but when you have to constantly go through pain at the hands of wicked and evil people including spirits then you become broken and I am broken. I did it all on my own and despite my sister telling me I am strong I feel weak. I did not have to go through this I was telling her. I know Good God is there for me and with me, but there are times when all you want is to rest your head on his shoulders and he tells you you are going to be fine.**

My sister says she has it hard too, but yet I can't figure out how because husband and wife works and they make good money. She has financial issues also. Weird, but this is her life, she knows the trouble and troubles that's in it. As for me, I will always be alone and without because I was set this way. But with all this said, I am trying to overcome and conquer. I have to break her tie.

I was set to have nothing. All my prosperity is to be taken from me and to be honest, I am tired of God when it comes to this because he can't do a damned thing. No, I should not say that because like I've said, **he's been in**

the storm and storms with me. My hardships I've faced and have been victorious, but I am tired now because health wise and financial wise I am broken. I can't deal with the tying bullshit anymore. I need to untie myself but how is the question? How do I undo what he and she has done to me?

It's weird because I truly don't know why...........no let's not go into that because you don't have to do anything to anyone for them to hurt you.

Look at the different diseases man created to wipe out another race.

Look at the weapons man build to kill just to take another man's land and prosperity; wealth.

Look at the genocide that has happened throughout the centuries.

Look at the plagues throughout history that man carry into another man's land just to kill them and steal their land and resources.

Look at the theft through grave robbing that goes on throughout the ages. Man steal the bones of man and put them in museums; display. So not even the dead can rest in peace when it comes to modern day grave robbers.

Look at Chick V and or Chicken Gunya, West Nile, Ebola; modern day man made diseases that lame, meme and kill. All these things human's don't think of because to them hell does not exist, so they can do whatever they want to do. Human life and dignity is worth nothing. **<u>Therefore, the dollar bill and or money is valued over human life.</u>** Yes I get upset at God – Good God about this and class him as weak sometimes because he permits shit like this to happen.

At times I say death is stronger than him, hence people worship death and bow down to death. Trust me I truly don't want or need a weak god. I need strength. I need a god that is powerful so dat when evil come with dem bullshit im jus bax evil outta di wey splatow. No fam, evil get bax wey an slap wey. Evil haffi ole dem cheek an cry to di bax wey dem get. So yes I will forever be down on Good God for allowing evil to hurt and deceive his true people.

To me and for me, I truly love you, I am not expecting evil to come around me and or infiltrate my good up, good up home. As soon as evil and or wicked and evil people sey watchya man, si Michelle house dey, eee peaceful and mi a goh disrupt her peace and tranquility God step eene an sey, yu a goh wah and slap dem wey. Show them such terrible face dat dem flee forever ever. No evil should come to my door and

try anything. This is my boundaries and you should not cross it lest you get devoured.

I am not bothering you, so truly don't bother me because <u>**I am living by Psalms One that said, "blessed is the man that walketh not in the council of the ungodly"**</u>…….. Trust me I don't want or need to walk in the council of the ungodly nor do I want or need the ungodly around me. Stay the hell away from me and we will be fine. Don't take a penny from me either hence you will not like me. I don't take from you so you should not take from me. What I work hard for for Good God, myself, his land and lands including his good and true people, don't come tell me I have to pay you 30% of it for withholding fee. Yes I am upset that because my books are on Lulu.com the IRS withholds 30% of any revenue generated if the books are sold in the US. To me this is bullshit. I do not live in your country so don't tax me based on your ridiculous taxing schemes. I don't fund war nor do I accept the bullshit of your country when it comes to human rights. America violate their citizen's fundamental human, civil, religious and Good God given rights each and every day. All I have to do is look and point to the homelessness across the USA. So don't withhold what rightfully belongs to Good God and his people lest <u>**HE GOOD GOD TAX YOU. Trust me you withhold Good God's money, then he Good God has every right under the law and laws of life and death to withhold all from you. Don't mess with Good God and**</u>

what rightfully belongs to him. No land on the face of the earth can do this come on now. My romance line and or novels you can withhold taxes, but the Michelle Jean Books; this line you are entitled to nothing.

Yes when it comes to America, I can also point to the almost 1 trillion dollars per year that the government spend to fund Aries (War) whilst going against the code and law of life which is the upright eye in triangle that they have on some of their monetary notes. You are telling Good God you trust him, but yet fund Aries (War) and rob your people, economy and land of their blessings. **You lie to Good God daily because you do not trust him. If you did, Death would not speak of your land and its wickedness so openly in the spiritual realm. Hence America, the United States of America is no different from Jamaica, both lands are filthy, dirty.**

Hence life came to life and life rejected life. (Marcus Mosiah Garvey)

No land should tax the money I put away for them because it's not about taxes, it's about truth and the true and good blessings of Good God and Allelujah. If you need funds from this bank account no bank globally and no government globally can say, you can't get it because that money rightfully belongs to you. So if this account is in the Cayman Islands for which the account will be, the Cayman Islands cannot say, Russia you are not entitled to funds because you are.

The Cayman Islands cannot say British Columbia or Southern Africa with the exception of South Africa you are not entitled to funds because you are. Yes I will outline which lands in the Southern parts of Africa get funds. Uganda I am liking you hence I have to see about you. **<u>Yes Jamaica, if the land does not sink to the bottom of the ocean and or sea, I will have a special bank account for you.</u>** I truly love the land but I do not love or truly love the wicked and evil people. I refuse to support slackness and truly don't go there about me advertising Jamaican brands (artist). I'm a Jamaican no matter my descent, hence I am both spiritual and physical and I know the difference between the two.

You know what. I truly don't want to piss of Good God this morning, but I am going to ask yet again, Why the United States of America?

Yes I know the eye in the triangle, but why does she want me to go to New York?

What is so significant about New York that I have to go there?

Yes I know Marcus Mosiah Garvey went there but why me? I have no true desire to live in the United States even though it's Southern Land and this land claim the upright eye in triangle.

Yes true life people.

America can boast on this because the upright eye in triangle represent final life; true life. Once you have the upright triangle and or get the upright eye in triangle you have true live and you go up to see Good God and Allelujah. Yes symbolism plays an intricate part in spirituality and if you truly don't know about symbolism then you are lost; doomed.

Some people point the triangle down and this is fine. All they are telling me and Good God is that they've accepted spiritual death for themselves. Death is their god and this is fine. Therefore, death have to save them not me if I am the saving grace for humanity.

Well the Satanist has the five pointed star and the goat head or whatever animal they call it and this is fine; they worship and praise wrong. They know not what they worship and praise. **_I know they worship and praise female death not male death. She is more powerful than male death but yet they don't know this._** When you can stop male death you cannot stop female death because she is the more destructive of the two. **_She takes everything in sight and it matters not if you are good or evil._** Female death is the one you truly do not want to piss off because she is that deadly. She can sink your land without remorse. What belongs to her belongs to her and you do not interfere with it; her. Hence many messengers have and has gone to their deaths because of her. Therefore I tell you to live by Psalms One and leave the devil and his children alone.

So female death is represented by the five pointed star and male death is represented by the six pointed star.

But

Don't go there because you are not confused. Spread the man apart and look at him.

2 heads; one up and the other down
2 arms
2 legs

Add

Total is 6.

Where's the two heads?

His head that points up and his penis that points down.

Yes ooh.

Female

One head
Two arms
Two legs

But the vagina?

Receives him. He goes up into her. Yes I know some say down but either way he's the giver and she's the receiver. Therefore she has the womb, the womb and cradle of life. She brings forth life and not him. And it matters not if the life she brings forth is good or evil. **<u>She's the caregiver and giver of life. Hence it is imperative that women do not lay with unclean humans and spirit.</u>**

You can't lay with spirits.

YES YOU CAN, YOU JUST DON'T KNOW HOW TO.
That's Ludicrous.

No it's not.

Spirits do lay with humans. Ask a true Jamaican or African or a person from the Caribbean like Trinidad, Grenada, Haiti and St. Lucia but I am not sure about St. Lucia.

But you are invoking the dead.

You do not have to invoke the dead for the dead to sleep with you. And yes I am so off topic because I was talking about money, the money I will put away for Good God and his land and people.

No, I do not have a desire to save the United States but deep down my spirit is saying otherwise on this day and I truly don't know why.

Maybe I found the mansion I wanted to give Good God in Atlanta Georgia but because Atlanta is prostitute vile I said no. Lap dances people hence the dirty South; the racism and shit that go on behind closed doors in the south. And no one better ask me why Southerners are so damned racist. We truly don't like outsiders. This is our world, don't come and taint it or try to filthy it; hence you will not like the consequences.

No come to think of it, Southerners are frigging racist. Damn don't even say it because reality is hitting. And it's not ya think.

This shit is engrained in our spiritual DNA. Damn because you can't get it out. No wonder some Southerners inbreed. Shit this is bad.

Sorry people but this is sad but is it?

I'm still not budging; hence Psalms One will do for me more than infinitely and indefinitely forever ever without end. Truly love my Southern Men. Damn they're fat and gorgeous. Just the way I like em.

Okay I better stop because I am way too off topic.

It's March 22 and the dreams are coming.

Family I am dreaming in the past again. It's weird because I was in the past around 1865 and I could see fighting. So I don't know if females are going to die on prairie lands. I do not know if it's in Canada or the United States because I cannot tell you what outside looks like. Everything was inside but fighting and or death is coming on the prairies again.

Black children you are being warned. You have to start listening to good council and put down the gun. I have to start talking to the lots of you because you are truly children of the lost. **_Too much shit is happening in the black community and you need to_**

take heed and start changing the way you think about life.

Remember governments did not create ghettos we did. We allowed wicked and evil people to infiltrate our society; hence drugs, alcohol and all manner of diseases are prevalent in black communities. This bullshit has to stop. If mama and daddy is strung out on drugs how are they going to raise you?

If you are strung out on drugs, how are you going to be productive in the community that you live in?

How are you productive to yourself?
Are you not killing yourself?

Stop being labelled as ghetto and stop saying you are from the ghetto because no human being is slum. We turn where we live in into slums; hence we take on the slum and or ghetto mentality.

Regression is a sin come on now.

You cannot continually regress, you will amount to nothing.

Well I sell drugs and I'm making it.

You are still in the projects hence you've not made it.

You do not have a house nor do you have a major bank account.

You are on the lookout for the police.

The feds are tracking you despite some of you working for the feds; them.

Everyone needs to progress in life and if you can't you are doomed. Listen it's time the black man and child wake up because when it's all said and done, hell has no colour barriers or colour scheme. Once you get there you will all be one colour because you have to take on the colour of death; spiritual death and that's white. There are no ands ifs or buts about this. The colour of man – humanity represents death. I wouldn't even say Black is death because

Black Death does not kill the spirit, White Death does. Black Death just hand your spirit over to White Death for you to be sentenced to death in hell. Hell is where you serve your spiritual time before you die.

No, no, no, there's no I'm gonna or going to escape hell because you are sanctified and holy. Blood does not make you holy, it makes you dead. Blood is what humans accept hence humans live and die by the blood period. Humans are like vampires; you feast on blood and accept blood sacrifices.

So vampires and or vampirism is to death like humans are unto hell if this makes any sense.

<u>So black man, woman start changing lest you be told TOO LATE REAL SOON.</u>

Many of you say you are of African ancestry, well go back to Africa then. Find a home there and leave out of America because America doesn't want you. Southern lands must be cleansed and if collapsing these lands is the only way to get rid of some of you then yes it will be done. These lands will be destroyed.

Some of you blacks are saying you fear raising your children in America. So if you live in fear in a land that has no respect for you, what the hell are you doing raising your children there? You don't fear the land and or raising your child there because you continue to live like the ignorant; slaves then. Find a place and home you are comfortable in. Find that good and suitable environment to raise your child and or family come on now. Don't lie to me and tell me you fear raising your child and or children in American environment when you of yourself isn't actively looking for a better environment to live in.

Like I said, regression is a sin and it's time the black race stop living like the regressed and or the regressive. Africa is vast, go home, back to Africa and built the continent positively. Some of you are retired basketball and football players. Go to Africa and have an African Football or Basketball League and bring these sports to Africa. Play against the European League come on now.

Like I've said in some of my other books, if someone don't want you in their land, get the fuck out and take your resources with you. Build your own African own in a positive and good way. Come on now. Yes Africa and Africans need to straighten the fuck up and have some fucking ambition for self. Africa is the center and cradle of life; this world and universe and they disrespect her, and sell out Mother Africa. **Look at the**

bullshit that is happening on African soil. NOT ONE OF THESE AFRICAN NATIONS KNOW THAT FOR EVERY HUMAN THEY KILL, THEY ARE GIVING SATAN; DEATH THE VICOTORY OVER ALL OF AFRICA.

This is what evil wants hence EVIL POINTS AT GOOD GOD AND LAUGH BECAUSE OF OUR SELL OUT AFRICAN OWN. Good God gave them so much bountifully and instead of giving thanks, look at each African country and see what I see. Poverty and disgust all around due to war; greed. And come here with your propaganda bullshit and I will tell you how to use the fuck you sign up in you. I refuse to spread propaganda because like I said, Mama Africa is tired of the bullshit that is happening on African soil.

Off topic again

So family, I truly don't know what's going on. I truly don't know how to deal with the past. I also don't know what this prince has to do with me. He's royalty but I don't get it with me and why I am seeing his face. He's white but to me he's not modern but yet he's young. Is he showing me that I am of his family? But it matters not to me because of wrongs. How can I save him knowing the wrongs that some of them has done?

I know the dark past of Scotland because this darkness is engrained in me. My Scottish descendants I will save because Scotland is engrained in me, but not my English counterparts. I have no good will for England despite some of my descendants coming from there. Like I said, I am not only physical, I am spiritual and the spiritual is more powerful than the physical. This I will not expect any of you to comprehend.

There is a spiritual DNA but as humans we do not know this nor can we figure it out.

There is a great pull and I know the pull and sometimes you are caught in the middle of things, and in truth, I truly do not want to change me for anyone. I am me and I am going to stay me.

Yes the hosts of hell are against me, hence all the stops are being pulled out against me for me not to achieve my goal and destiny. But I cannot be bothered with evil on some days. I just have to live my life and stay away from wicked and evil people.

Evil must do all to maintain his and her people and anyone that is good is a threat to evil, hence I am. Evil do not want to lose a soul but that's fine. I will have compassion for my Scottish descendants that were Kings and Queens before their legacy was stolen from them by the English. I have to remember them but I will not remember the wicked and evil ones. *Yes I know there is something there in Scottish history I do not know about in regards to lineage of Queen and Kingship, but one day I will find out the truth because as the present is important, so is our past.*

We have to know the past; the truth of the past before we can move forward and this I know now because I was told this in one of my visions this morning.

My journey now is finding out the truth of my Scottish past and or ancestry because something is truly not right. I truly do not know why I am seeing this regal prince in red and I think black but I know his jacket had red in it and he had black hair. He did not smile, he just had a solemn

look as if something is not complete in his life. There is something missing in his life. Maybe he's not even Scottish but yet he's showing me him.

There's a lot that I truly do not know hence I have to delve into my roots of the Gills; Gilfillan and the Clan Lyon and or Lyon (Lion) of Judah; the Judahites.

Like I've told Good God and Allelujah, I will not have anyone steal my identity. I am his child and I will not have anyone steal my name and heritage; that which rightfully belongs to me. I refuse it, hence he showed me the white woman hiding my ticket. My plane ticket to him and I will not have it. What rightfully belongs to me stays with me because it's mine and trust me you continue to take it, then there is infinitely going to be a problem. You are not of Lyon (s) so don't claim it because it's not yours. Step off and release Lyon (s) land (s) and people because we are the true Jews – Judahites come on now.

<u>**I know you not so truly don't take mine. There are people out there that knows the truth and it's time now for them to speak it. You cannot let frauds take what's rightfully yours come on now.**</u>

<u>**The truth can no longer be muzzled by wicked and evil people because they don't want to relinquish what rightfully do not belong to them. HENCE ANYONE THAT**</u>

MY TALK

<u>TRIES TO STEAL MY IDENTITY, HISTORY AND LINEAGE INCLUDING WEALTH (MONEY), I TRULY HOPE GOOD GOD AND ALLELUJAH PUNISH THEM WITH MORE THAN THE BOILS AND FIRES OF HELL MORE THAN INFINITELY AND INDEFINITELY FOREVER EVER WITHOUT END IN THE LIVING (PHYSICAL) AND SPIRITUAL WORLD.</u>

There is no place in Good God's kingdom and abode including land and lands for property thieves, monarch thieves, monetary thieves, identity thieves, culture thieves and what have you when it comes to thievery, lies, deceit, hate, sin and so forth.

What belongs to Good God and his people must be returned unto us lest everything you own be taken from you legally and rightfully so.

Don't steal from me and think it's going to be okay with Good God and Allelujah because brimstone and fire including hailstorms and thunderstorms must devour you; do their damage beyond repair infinitely and indefinitely forever

ever without end. I refuse you, so give me back what rightfully belongs to me come on now.

I take nothing from you, so don't take anything from me.

So no fam, I truly don't know about this monarchy; these people that are trying to get to me. I gather they are telling me that I have to put them on my docket of truth, but I truly don't know how to because I know not them and this is weird. Like I said, he did not say anything to me so I truly do not know what he wants me to do for him. Whatever truth that needs to be told hopefully one day he will lead me to it in goodness and in truth; true peace. I know there is more hence the 1800 hundreds play a significant part in my quest and or history of truth I take it.

Yes fam I truly don't know and maybe one day someone will put the pieces together for me for the world to truly see and know. And yes I am still dreaming about LA and my brother.

Michelle and Michelle Jean

It's March 23, 2015 and the more I see is the more disgusted I get with religion and man. I am so furious with God – Good God and Allelujah that I truly want to abandon him and say fuck it, let the chips fall where they may because he's of no fucking use to me.

No Fam, I am bent because so much have and has been done to the black man and or race that we've become so fucking stupid when it comes to our true story and heritage that it is beyond me.

Good God gave us a name and way of life and instead of embracing it we readily accept the crap and shit of the different religions of the globe. Crap and shit that is taken from our culture and true story that has been watered down to reflect these fucking identity thieves.

Family, I am so bend that I so want to knock every black man and woman and stamp fucking idiotic morons on their foreheads. Why the fuck are we embracing

religion when religion kill and rob the black man and woman including child of their ancestral life story; true life?

Have we become that fucking stupid that we do not know where we are from anymore?

WHITE SOCIETY CAN NO LONGER TAKE THE BLACK MAN AND OR THE BLACK RACES IDENTITY AND SAY IT IS HIS BECAUSE IT IS NOT. NOR CAN THE BLACK SOCIETY TAKE THE WHITE MAN OR RACES IDENTITY AND SAY IT IS HIS; OURS.

They are two different hues based on the Ying and Yang and or the universe. Yes this is also death, how the flesh is returned to the earth and how the spirit dies.

<u>Because we are human beings, all is shown to us in human form.</u> As humans we cannot comprehend the spiritual nor do we know about the spiritual. We live for flesh and fleshy things not spiritual things hence sight is given in fleshy and or human form. We dream and get visions in human and or fleshy form because that's all we know. Hence hue is taken to the spiritual realm for humans and not animals per say.

So to every race globally, stop fucking stealing the black man's heritage. Get and have your fucking own if you can. I am fucking tired of you raping us and selling us watered down crap of our heritage and we as foolish black people based on hue keep buying the shit that is leading and taking us straight to hell.

STOP FUCKING CALLING YOURSELF ISRAELITE HEBREWS TOO. YOU'RE NOT FUCKING DEAD NOR ARE YOU OF THE HOUSE OF THE DEAD. THERE ARE NO FUCKING BLACK HEBREWS.

No I should not say that because Ethiopia keep Israel and some of you dead ass fucking idiotic black morons keep the Israelite bullshit going.

If God hates these people because they joined forces with Satan long before Eve why are you continuing with the Israelic trend? Morons and idiots if you are not a Jew – Judahite there is no way that you are going to see Good God. Know that and weep. NO ISRAELITE CAN GO TO GOOD GOD PERIOD. THEY ARE NOT ACCEPTED AND NEVER WILL BE ACCEPTED BECAUSE ISRAEL, THE TRUE ISRAELITES SOLD OUT GOOD GOD LONG BEFORE ADAM AND EVE AND THIS IS WHY MANY BLACK PEOPLE WE

ENSLAVED. WE KEEP SELLING OUT OUR OWN TO THE FUCKING BABYLONIANS.

Ethiopia is the land of the Ethers hence it's the land of sin; the fire people and or the people of smokeless fire. Know your fucking history and the true truth.

Like Marcus Mosiah Garvey said, a people without knowledge of his history are like trees without roots. Meaning we are dead hence REVELATIONS SAID, WE ARE THE FIRST BEGOTTEN OF THE DEAD. We know nothing but yet claim to be. Stop being fucking fooled and wake the fuck up.

ISRAEL, THE ORIGINAL ISRAELITES ABANDONED GOOD GOD AND ALLELUJAH HENCE THEY HAVE NO PLACE WITH HIM SO WHY ARE YOU CARRYING ON THE TREND?

Hebrew is not the language of God – Good God and Allelujah.

Arabic is not the language of God – Good God and Allelujah.

No language on the face of this planet comes close to the language of Good God. This language heals, it turns back evil, cure, connects you to Good God directly, so I truly don't know that the hell you fraudulent black people are doing.

Religion is not of Good God nor is Israel.

Israel can never ever be of Good God because Israel let him go long ago. Know the truth of you and your true lineage; true story not HIS STORY (HISTROY); what he tells you.

All of you know the name of Good God but yet give him bullshit names like Jesus and Yahweh and Jehovah.

<u>*Allelujah is the proper name of Good God because it's the name the spirit cries out to when the energy of your spirit is hit the right way.*</u> Both good and evil cry out this name hence those bullshit life rapists that call themselves Muslim use Allah. <u>*They cannot say Allelujah because the fullness of Good God and Allelujah is truly not with them. They rape and massacre Life hence killing the Breath of Life each and every day.*</u>

So yes I am angry and fed up of the bullshit that is happening globally and yes I cuss the black race good and proper because this morning I refuse to cuss Lovey, I have *to cuss the black race because we are the ones that are the stupid ones.*

We claim African lineage but yet know not the watered down crap of our lineage that is being fed to us to keep us ignorant and stupid.

They call us slaves, say we came from slaves. Who the fuck are they to tell us this? We are the ones to create this universe and world, so truly go fuck yourselves with the slavery bullshit. Good God did not make slaves, man; human beings turn each other into slaves.

You the ignorant and fool fool black people can stand up and say you are descendants of slaves, but I refuse to anymore because I know the full and true truth of my lineage and descent.

You as black people want to be identified as slaves, so keep your damned slave trend.

Keep your damned slave mentality also. Do not give it to me because I don't want or need to continue with the black and stupid slave trend.

You keep being the ignorant and stupid you and I will continue to cuss your ass and do me.

I want no part of your slavery bullshit. Keep it and keep turning yourselves down with it. I am looking up hence Good God and Allelujah is who I know and walk with; devote myself to.

We can no longer let people steal our identity and say it is theirs when it is truly not theirs.

Fuck off man and stop stealing from Black People.

Don't fucking steal our GOD and say our God is your god if you hate us so. Don't fucking taint our God either because he's not fucking dead, nor is he Jesus – Zeus and or Heysuis. You rape us of everything then turn around and fuck us. Who the fuck are you to do this?

Pussy hole lef wi alone and find your own fucking useless and murderous god and gods. THE BLACK MAN'S GOD AND OR THE TRUE BLACK RACES GOD IS NOT

YOURS, SO FUCKING LEAVE HIM THE FUCK ALONE.

FUCK OFF AND LEAVE THE FUCKING BLACK RACE THE FUCK ALONE BECAUSE I AM SO FUCKING BENT THAT I CAN'T CUSS GOOD GOD RUDE MI AFFI CUSS UNNU.

You don't fucking like us then don't fucking use us. This is the hierarchy of the mountain of God – Good God and Allelujah.

- Level One: Chinese and Blacks – this is the level I chose.

- Level Two: Whites alone. On this level you find sickness, sick white people. So this is where Sikhism comes in. To be a Seik means you are sickly. Hence you the white race have been robbed of your identity by the so called Hindu's and or Babylonians of India.

- Level Three: All black people. This level I did not like though I can go from level one to level three without issues and problems.

The only race I did not see on this mountain is the Spanish and Indian and or Hindu race. And like I said in some of my other books, this is how I saw it and this is how I am relating it back to humanity.

It's amazing how billions of us say we belong when we truly do not belong. Family and Good God I am truly sorry because I am tired of these fucking Babylonians stealing that which belongs to us, the true Jews come on now.

Who the fuck are they to say they are Jews when they are not?

Who the fuck are the Babylonian Jews?
They are not Jews.

<u>We don't interlock the triangles because a TRUE JEW know that this is wrong and an abomination of sin and a true abomination unto Good God.</u>

The TRUE JEWS ARE TO HAVE NOTHING TO DO WITH BABYLON. HENCE A TRUE JEW CANNOT MARRY ANYONE IN THE ISLAMIC FAITH. IT IS MORE THAN TRULY AND UNCONDITIONALLY FORBIDDEN FOREVER EVER. AND THIS HAS NOTHING TO DO WITH SKIN TONE BUT HAS EVERYTHING TO DO WITH LIES AND DECEIT.

BABYLON'S GOD IS NOT JEWISH GOD COME ON NOW.

Good God's children cannot have anything to do with Satan's children and we all know this but we choose to live in lies anyway.

The interlocking triangles are death, so why do you permit this. The True Jews are females of black and white lineage.

They are also black.
They are also white hence your mountain is the way it is. Therefore, the mountains of earth will always represent the upward triangle.

As humans we all have choices and the choice we make as well as the life we live on earth determines where we go in the afterlife; meaning when the spirit shed the flesh.

Yes you can laugh all you want but Good God has and have been trying to save humanity for more than centuries, but instead of choosing life we choose death and die. Humans were not suppose to die. We were to go back to Good God whole and or as one. Meaning flesh and spirit were to walk to Good God as one and continue to live, but because of sin we cannot do this.

We keep polluting ourselves and expect him Good God to swoop down and clean up our mess. And I keep telling you, Good God is not a fucking Molly Maid to come in and clean up our messes. We make them (the mess) so we have to clean them come on now. Yes he shows us what to do via his messengers but how many of us truly listen. We listen to others tell us bullshit and when it's too late we cry to Good God and say he's not fair. Slavery did not have to be for many black people but as Blacks we too do not listen. We do not keep our life clean. We would rather live dirty and lose our place with Good God instead of coming clean and living clean.

Yes I am tired of the bullshit because many people know the full truth but keep their damned mouths shut.

Yes I am bent because the truth should never be muzzled. You have the truth now so if you want to say I am lying so be it. Like I said, I refuse to tell anyone to accept my Lovey and more than delicious God. I should not have to because we should know him.

Yes I face turmoil but look at Job in your Illuminati book and or Free Mason book of death; your so called holy bible. That book steal the lineage of the Black race and perverted it, hence they turn around and give you sin, sell you sin. Hence Good God and Allelujah knows beyond a shadow of a doubt that I do not stand for identity thieves and anyone say they are going to steal my history and lineage, including the lineage of my people then he Good God knows to truly rain down fire and brimstone of the worst kind, including hailstorms and thunderstorms on these people or the person that does immediately. Don't wait but mash dem up and dem lan because I am not fucking into it. Don't steal from me nor take what is rightfully mine.

Don't steal from me. And when I am dead meaning the spirit leaves the body, don't come rape my bones either. Truss mi, any man, woman or child including spirit come interfere with my grave knows that dem head a guh tun behind dem immediately. Mek mi ress in peace. Don't interfere with me. Clean my burial spot and make sure I have my garden with roses, nice flowers, but don't interfere with my grave site in any other way come on now.

If you want to come and just look at my burial site this is fine, but don't dirty it or come with any stinking bullshit because I will not have it. I will lift you off your feet and toss you down. And trust me many dead has and have done this to human beings in the living, but they just don't know it. It happened to me. But then the little boy warned me of this before it happened. Mi guh step pan duppy head and get knock the fuck down. So don't think that the dead hath not power, they do until all is over and that is before 2032.

So to religion I say, Fuck You because religion kills. Hence billions are in hell already because of religious bullshit and the bullshit of religion.

<u>Yes Good God is energy that which you call spirit, BUT BECAUSE ALL WE KNOW IS THE FLESH AND NOT SPIRIT, HE HAS TO SHOW US EVERYTHING IN THE FLESH INCLUDING HIM. WHEN WE SIN WE RELINQUISH ALL RIGHTS TO SEE HIM IN HIS TRUE FORM AND OR STATE. This is what humanity fail to see and or realize until this day.</u>

So yes I am pissed off when I see people stealing the black man's lineage, true story and heritage. Like I said, the black race is White and Black including Chinese hence no other race should come and steal from us.

And yes not all Whites and Black including Chinese belong to the black race. And yes you can go by lands if you have to. Hence the separation of lands must be completed. Once this happen, many lands will be destroyed if not wiped off the face of the plant. Therefore I've told you the extinction of man – humanity is before 2032. We lost 2132 and rightfully so because the wickedness and thievery of man – humans have gone on for far too long.

We care not hence the devil and his people are making sure the lands of earth become uninhabitable for Good God's true people including Good God himself.

<u>*Billions have lost their souls and can't redeem it because of the bullshit of religion and the sins that we as individuals do each and every day.*</u>

Like I said, we cannot sin and think we won't be paid for the sins that we do. As humans we think in human form and not in spiritual form. Yes we can think in both hence I've told you, <u>my biggest fear is losing Good God.</u> I do not want to do anything that is displeasing to him. I also do not want to live on pins and needles when it comes to him, hence I live by my standards, that which is right in my book. <u>I know for a fact that if I am wrong he will tell me I am wrong.</u> Hence I rely on him for everything.

<u>MAN KILL, GOOD GOD DOES NOT KILL.</u>

Man tell us lies to follow so that we can go to hell with them and die, and this is sad.

Man tell lies on Good God but oh what a day for them because many are going to weep and moan in hell shortly, and yes we as humans are going to hear them. Bob Marley told you, "there's a natural mystic blowing in the air and if you listen carefully you will hear." He's not lying but this time around you are going to hear the dead cry literally. The only reason why we don't hear right now is because of the traffic, whether that traffic be musical noise, airplanes, buses, cars, vans, crying, fighting, barking; you name it.

The cries of man will be heard shortly because man has and have become more than vile and wicked in the sight of him Good God and Man.

<u>*Death's people have to take and they are taking. See with the children of death they think they can't be redeemed.* **BUT EVERYONE CAN BE REDEEMED.**</u>

YES YOU HEARD ME RIGHT.

EVERYONE CAN BE REDEEMED, BUT IT'S NOT MANY THAT WANT TO.

<u>**TRUTH IS EVERLASTING LIFE, HENCE WE MUST WALK AND TALK IN TRUTH NOT LIES. LIES GET US AND OR BRING US TO HELL, BUT TRUTH GIVE US EVERLASTING AND OR ETERNAL LIFE WITH GOOD GOD.**</u>

Like I've told you in some of my other books, there is no water in hell and our spirit needs water. This is why when we ask for blessings from Good God he showers us with water. Water *is a blessing because water is life. Without water; the waters of life you are dead; will die.*

This too is why I cannot comprehend or over stand why anyone would want to die to go to hell knowing that there is no water there, and the spirit is going to go thirsty; die a slow and agonizing death.

Imagine spending trillions of years in hell wanting water and can't get none. This is why I tell you, I don't want to be no politician.

Imagine the debt you've inherited as a government leader. Then on top of that, you might incur more debt on top of the debt your inherited.

Lord have mercy because your debts do add up not just monetarily but through death as well. Yes through death because many of you send your citizens to fight wars; battles that do not concern your nation. So add the debt of that nation on top of your debt as well. Trust me your hell will be so dark and painful that the demons of hell are going to need a special light just to see you. (Black Holes)

Remember I told you, your sins are like the tattooed eye; hence tattoos are sins and many of you, billions have your sins walking around in human form. Wow I can just imagine what your sins look like in hell.

<u>So truly good luck to billions of you because if you are not right with Good God on earth you can never be right with him in the grave.</u> AND LIKE I SAID, IF I AM THE SAVING GRACE FOR HUMANITY, I REFUSE TO SAVE ANY WICKED AND EVIL PEOPLE. TRUST ME DEATH KNOWS I WILL NOT STAND IN THEIR WAY AGAIN FROM TAKING WHAT'S RIGHTFULLY THEIRS.

I WILL NOT SACRIFICE MY LIFE FOR NO WICKED AND EVIL PEOPLE BECAUSE I KNOW THE WICKEDNESS OF WICKED AND EVIL PEOPLE AND SPIRITS; HENCE I PETITION GOOD GOD AND ALLELUJAH FOR NONE. GO THE FUCK TO HELL AND BURN. WHEN YOU WERE DOING ALL YOUR WICKEDNESS AND EVIL HERE ON EARTH AND IN

THE SPIRITUAL REALM, YOU DID NOT THINK OF THE HURT AND PAIN YOU WERE CAUSING THAT PERSON INCLUDING CHILD. SO WHY THE HELL WOULD I PRESERVE AND OR RESERVE A PLACE FOR YOU WITH GOOD GOD AND ALLELUJAH COME ON NOW?

<u>So if the black race want to keep sacrificing themselves to death so be it. **DO NOT SELL ME DEATH, YOUR BLACK AND WHITE JESUS BECAUSE I KNOW WHAT DEATH LOOKS LIKE, HENCE I KNOW THEM; KNOW DEATH.** So because I know death, I walk away from death because death cannot save me, death can only kill me. (Jesus)</u>

Sin not and you will have a place with him, but for some of you, it's already too late. Like I said, do not steal what rightfully belongs to the Black Race (not based on hue) and think you are going to get away with it.

I refuse to hate based on hue but I will cuss you to scorn if you continue to take what is rightfully ours. Our God is not your god, so truly step off and find your decrepit own; dead own.

Your God is death so find death and truly leave life alone. Don't pollute our water, don't drink it either.

Don't eat our food and marry our men and women either.

And yes it's time for the BLACK RACE (not based on hue) TO HAVE SOME FUCKING AMBITION. ABSOLUTELY NO ONE CAN TAKE RACE (BASED ON HUE AND OR COLOUR OF SKIN) TO GOOD GOD AND ALLELUJAH.

NO ONE CAN TAKE THIS BULLSHIT TO THE UNIVERSE EITHER. YOU WILL ALL BE REJECTED AND RIGHTFULLY SO BECAUSE LIFE IS A MIXTURE OF RACE; EVERYTHING.

Hence I've told you no one can say God or Good God I am black and you belong to me. They will not see Good God's door. You will forever be trying to find and can't find it. And yes this is what's happened to billions of us today as well. We keep seeking and cannot find. Energy; pure energy is not a colour, hence many of you cannot comprehend the darkness – the blackness of the light. There is light in the darkness hence Good God and his angels and messengers we cannot see.

<u>There is life in the darkness hence the light comprehended it not. So because we cannot see, **HE GOOD GOD AND ALLELUJAH MUST GIVE YOU THINGS IN THE IMAGE THAT YOU CAN SEE IN.**</u>

Like I said, because we are human Good God gives us knowledge in human form. He cannot give us knowledge in spiritual form because we've lost our way and we know not the spiritual realm.

We cannot see true spirits hence there is a major difference between ghosts and spirits. And yes we've intertwined the two for you to understand and this is wrong but this is the way it must be for now.

Michelle and Michelle Jean

So to the Netherlands, please guard your children because something is to happen to them. I truly don't know if it's death. But I know there was a sickly child that needed me but I could not reach her. But I think I reached her in the end. So please save guard your healthcare and children. I cannot fully tell you what's to happen because I truly don't know. Hence I am telling you to safe guard your children because sickness is looming.

America I don't know what I am going to do with you because I keep dreaming about you and dead people.

This morning March 26, 2015 I dreamt Sherman Hemsley in brown. In the dream I knew him and I was telling him he was in the show. The show is like the show Empire that's on television right now. But in the dream we were talking about another show. He was telling me he could help me. But people I did not pay him any mind because he's dead and I knew he was dead. He did not know he was dead from the looks of it but I knew he was. Also, what stood out about him was his nose. He had this huge nose that was not his, hence I took him with a grain of salt.

So yes I am dreaming about American men both living and dead and I truly don't know why.

Plus I am dreaming about the land and or country more and more.

Yes there are more dreams but I can't truly tell you them because I truly don't remember them. My concern right now is with the children of the globe because we are messing them up and this is sad.

Listen, I will not talk about a wakeup call because every book in the Michelle Jean Series of Books should be your wake up call. We are on the path way of destruction shortly; hence my woes have gone up to Good God. I truly do not care about wicked and evil people, including wicked and evil societies and spirits because all that is wicked and evil must come tumbling down. As humans we refuse to listen to the truth hence religion deceives us so.

Religion lie to us so and we gobble it up. Hence Psalms One all the way for me.

So as I vent, truly good luck to humanity because the devil's children in going to make many of you pay and they are doing this right now. I will not fear them hence I rebuke them all globally in the name of Good God and Allelujah. They are done; dead to me truthfully.

<u>Trust me they are going to make you weep and moan because we were to lock them out but we keep letting them in through the back door.</u>

Africa, Nigeria truly woe be unto you because you practice and participate in death hence Death truly loves you. You massacre your own for death. KNOW THIS, NIGERIA, EVERY NIGERIAN IS GOING TO PAY BECAUSE NO MAN WOMAN OR CHILD SHOULD TAKE THE UPRIGHT TRIANGLE OF LIFE AND DESTROY IT.

Good God gave Africa his womb of life; life itself and you are destroying it without mercy; care.

Your people take life brutally and for this every Nigerian no matter descent must walk alone. Trust me all your names be taken out of the book of life. YOU DO NOT SHAME AND DISGRACE MAMA AFRICA LIKE THIS. SHE'S TIRED AND YOU CONTINUE TO KILL HER FOR BABYLON. YOU KNOW DIFFERENTLY BUT YET SIDE WITH DEATH AGAINST YOUR OWN. SO AS YOU DO THIS TO YOUR PEOPLE, I NOW TAKE TRUE LIFE FROM YOU AND LEAVE YOU TO YOUR OWN DEMISE AND DESTRUCTION. Mama Africa is worth it and you've accepted death for your land and people. So unto death must all of you go no matter where in the globe you all live. I give you no redemption because you did not have to do this to her Mama Africa. Come on now. Look at Africa and her skin and tell me why you do this to Mama, the womb and cradle of all life including universal life?

Yes America has the eye in triangle but once the last of the TRUE JEWS FIND THEIR HOME, THAT LAND WILL BE DESTROYED. Must be destroyed because they say they stand with God but yet kill God; spend hundreds of billions to keep war;

Aries going. Hence truly woe be unto them for the lies they tell and the lives they kill; take daily.

America; the United States of America is locked in hell hence Good God will always send his children into Babylon to get his good and true people out. Once his people are out they must stay out infinitely and indefinitely forever ever without end.

Michelle and Michelle Jean

OTHER BOOKS BY MICHELLE JEAN

Blackman Redemption – The Fall of Michelle Jean
Blackman Redemption – After the Fall Apology
Blackman Redemption – World Cry – Christine Lewis
Blackman Redemption
Blackman Redemption – The Rise and Fall of Jamaica
Blackman Redemption – The War of Israel
Blackman Redemption – The Way I Speak to God
Blackman Redemption – A Little Talk With Man
Blackman Redemption – The Den of Thieves
Blackman Redemption – The Death of Jamaica
Blackman Redemption – Happy Mother's Day
Blackman Redemption – The Death of Faith
Blackman Redemption – The War of Religion
Blackman Redemption – The Death of Russia
Blackman Redemption – The Truth
Blackman Redemption – Spiritual War
Blackman Redemption – The Youths
Blackman Redemption – Black Man Where Is Your God?

The New Book of Life
The New Book of Life – A Cry For The Children
The New Book of Life – Judgement
The New Book of Life – Love Bound
The New Book of Life – Me
The New Book of Life – Life

Just One of Those Days
Book Two – Just One of Those Days
Just One of Those Days – Book Three The Way I Feel
Just One of Those Days – Book Four

MY TALK

The Days I Am Weak
Crazy Thoughts – My Book of Sin
Broken
Ode to Mr. Dean Fraser

A Little Little Talk
A Little Little Talk – Book Two

Prayers
My Collective
A Little Talk/A Time For Fun and Play
Simple Poems
Behind The Scars
Songs of Praise And Love

Love Bound
Love Bound – Book Two

Dedication Unto My Kids
More Talk
Saving America From A Woman's Perspective
My Collective the Other Side of Me
My Collective the Dark Side of Me
A Blessed Day
Lose To Win
My Doubtful Days – Book One

My Little Talk With God
My Little Talk With God – Book Two

A Different Mood and World – Thinking

My Nagging Day
My Nagging Day – Book Two
Friday September 13, 2013
My True Love
It Would Be You
My Day

A Little Advice – Talk
1313, 2032, 2132 – The End of Man
Tata

MICHELLE'S BOOK BLOG – BOOKS 1 – 20

My Problem Day
A Better Way
Stay – Adultery and the Weight of Sin – Cleanliness Message

Let's Talk
Lonely Days – Foundation
A Little Talk With Jamaica – As Long As I Live
Instructions For Death
My Lonely Thoughts
My Lonely Thoughts – Book Two
My Morning Talks – Prayers With God
What A Mess
My Little Book
A Little Word With You
My First Trip of 2015
Black Mother – Mama Africa
Islamic Thought
My California Trip January 2015
My True Devotion by Michelle – Michelle Jean

My Many Questions To God